SCH
3-2018

2017

DATE DUE

W9-BQI-167

OUR DIGITAL PLANET

How Computers Work

by Ben Hubbard

capstone

Edited by Nikki Potts
Designed by Sarah Bennett
Picture research by Ruth Smith
Production by Laura Manthe
Originated by Capstone Global Library Limited
Printed and bound in China
007875

Library of Congress Cataloging-in-Publication Data
Names: Hubbard, Ben, 1973- author.
Title: How computers work / by Ben Hubbard.
Description: North Mankato, Minnesota : Heinemann Raintree, a Capstone imprint, [2017] | Series: Heinemann read and learn. Our digital planet |Audience: Ages 6-8. | Audience: K to grade 3. | Includes bibliographical references and index.
Identifiers: LCCN 2016029366| ISBN 9781484635988 (library binding) | ISBN 9781484636022 (pbk.) | ISBN 9781484636145 (ebook (pdf))
Subjects: LCSH: Computers--Juvenile literature. | Computer science--Juvenile literature.
Classification: LCC QA76.52 .H83 2017 | DDC 004--dc23
LC record available at https://lccn.loc.gov/2016029366

Acknowledgements
We would like to thank the following for permission to reproduce photographs: Getty Images: ERIC PIERMONT/AFP, 21; Shutterstock: Africa Studio, 22 (touchscreen), Aleksandar Grozdanovski, 7, 22 (chip), back cover right, Andrey_Popov, 19, Catalin Petolea, 20, Dario Lo Presti, 22 (circuit), FabrikaSimf, 17, Georgejmclittle, 22 (WiFi), Makaule, 8, Mark Agnor, 22 (trackpad), Monkey Business Images, 5, narinbg, 22 (hard drive), Nikolaeva, cover design element, interior design element, Piotr Adamowicz, 6, Pressmaster, 12, 14, ProStockStudio, cover, rawcaptured photography, 9, Rawpixel.com, 15, 18, sirikorn thamniyom, 16, Stefano Carocci Ph, 10, back cover left, Syda Productions, 4, vtwinpixel, 11, wavebreakmedia, 13

We would like to thank Matt Anniss for his invaluable help in the preparation of this book.

Every effort has been made to contact copyright holders of material reproduced in this book. Any omissions will be rectified in subsequent printings if notice is given to the publisher.

All the internet addresses (URLs) given in this book were valid at the time of going to press. However, due to the dynamic nature of the internet, some addresses may have changed, or sites may have changed or ceased to exist since publication. While the author and publisher regret any inconvenience this may cause readers, no responsibility for any such changes can be accepted by either the author or the publisher.

Contents

Some words are shown in bold, **like this**.
You can find them in the glossary on page 22.

Where Do We Find Computers?

Computers are all around us: in our schools, workplaces, and homes. Many homes have a computer, such as a laptop or tablet.

Others have a smart phone, which is also a computer. Computers don't all look the same, but they are made from similar parts.

What Is Hardware?

A computer is made of many parts. They are called **hardware**. On the outside, computer hardware may include a screen, keyboard, mouse, or **trackpad**.

On the inside, hardware includes **chips** and **circuit** boards.

What Are Chips and Circuit Boards?

Chips and **circuit** boards are a computer's brain. The most important circuit board is the "motherboard."

central processing unit (CPU)

The motherboard contains the
computer's most powerful chip.
This chip controls all the other chips.
It is called the Central Processing
Unit (CPU).

How Is Memory Stored?

hard drive

A computer stores most information and programs on a **hard drive**. Information is also stored on **chips**. These chips are called ROM (Read Only Memory) and RAM (Random Access Memory).

RAM

ROM holds information whether or not the computer is on. RAM holds information only while the computer is on.

What Is Input?

The information we give a computer is called "input."

We can give a computer information in many ways. We can use tools such as a keyboard, mouse, microphone, or **touchscreen**.

What Is Processing?

A computer uses its CPU and memory to complete tasks. The CPU follows the instructions we give it.

The CPU also follows instructions from programs. This is called "processing."

What Is Output?

When a computer has finished a task, it provides the results. A screen, printer, or headphones can all give results.

These results are called "outputs."
Print-outs and music are types of output.

Do Computers Talk To Each Other?

Computers not only send information to humans, but also to other computers. Computers connect though the Internet.

The Internet is a system that connects computers throughout the world. We usually access the Internet by connecting our smart phones, tablets, and laptops to **WiFi**.

How Fast Are Computers?

Modern personal computers can process inputs and produce outputs almost instantly. Supercomputers are even faster.

These great machines can complete trillions of tasks every second. Supercomputers are used by large companies.

Glossary

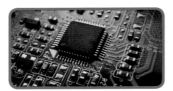

chip also called a "microchip;" a chip is a tiny circuit on a thin slice of plastic

circuit path that carries an electrical signal

hard drive also called a "hard disk;" a hard drive stores memory

touchscreen type of computer that allows a user to choose options by touching the screen

trackpad also called a "touchpad;" a trackpad is a surface that a user slides his or her fingers across to control the onscreen pointer

WiFi wireless Internet connection

Find Out More

Books

Aloian, Sam. *How a Computer Is Made.* Engineering Our World. New York: Gareth Stevens Publishing, 2016.

Peterson, Megan Cooley. *The First Computers.* Famous Firsts. North Mankato, Minn.: Capstone Press, 2015.

Yearling, Tricia. *Computers: What They Are and How to Use Them.* Zoom in on Technology. New York: Enslow Publishing, 2016.

Internet Sites

Facthound offers a safe, fun way to find Internet sites related to this book. All of the sites on Facthound have been researched by our staff.

Here's all you do:
Visit *www.facthound.com*
Type in this code: 9781484635988

Index